Delicious
Days! Any Your Name

THE CHAKRAS AND CRYSTALS COOKBOOK

Also by
Amy Leigh Mercree

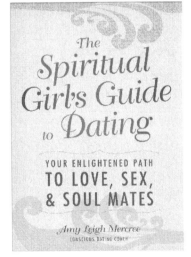

THE CHAKRAS AND CRYSTALS COOKBOOK

Juices, Sorbets, Smoothies, and Salads
to Empower Your Energy Centers

by Amy Leigh Mercree

Cover Photographer: Keri Johnson
Cover Design: Shannon Kaiser
Interior Design: Chad Mercree

DEDICATION

This book is dedicated to the plant beings, animals, and stone beings of the Earth. May they live feeling respected and loved.

ACKNOWLEDGMENTS

I'd like to thank Chad Mercree for the amazing internal design and production work on the book and Shannon Kaiser for the spectacular cover design. My agent Lisa Hagan is always a wonderful cheerleader. Thank you to everyone who has sampled my recipes and provided feedback. I am forever grateful for my loving family, friends, and supportive husband.

DISCLAIMER

Please note: Amy is not a doctor. Always consult with your physician before making any health decisions. Please understand that "The Chakras and Crystals Cookbook: Juices, Sorbets, Smoothies and Salads to Empower Your Energy Centers" by Amy Leigh Mercree is not a physician/patient relationship with you, so it will not provide a medical diagnosis, prescribe medicine, give psychotherapy or be reimbursable by medical insurance.

You are at all times responsible for your own safety. Mercree may offer suggestions and ideas to consider applying in your life but you are responsible for all of your choices, actions, decisions, and your own mental, physical, spiritual, and emotional health.

Enjoy!
Love,
Amy
XO

Table of Contents

INTRODUCTION

Welcome to *The Chakras and Crystals Cookbook*! I'm so happy that you stopped by! I wrote this book because I love juicing. And I love to make sorbets and smoothies and invent new salads. I think food should be fun and creative and colorful. Nutrition should be a creative, holistic, even ecstatic process. Who says healthy eating has to be boring?

So, why chakras and crystals? I'm glad you asked! In my bestselling book, *A Little Bit of Chakras: An Introduction to Energy Healing*, my husband Chad and I explored the amazing healing power of chakras. As an artistic, creative person the appeal of an array of chakra colors in my diet was irresistible. It just so happens that we can identify parts of our bodies that could use a boost via our chakra energy centers and choose our food and beverages to energize our health. An array of hues in our food choices also leads to ingesting a super healthy variety of vitamins and minerals. Who wouldn't love that?

I created this cookbook so you can eat everything in the recipes if you are vegan. Every recipe also has alkalizing properties to raise your pH.

These recipes are appropriate for anti-candida diets. You may want to modify them a little bit by omitting most of the sugar containing fruits with the exception of lemons and limes.

Crystals are the fun cousins of mantras and mandalas. They fill our lives with gorgeous, sparkling light. I consider every crystal, stone, and seashell a living being, just like a plant or animal. I encourage you to find your own stones and crystals out in nature. Fill your home with their beauty. For the more rare and sparkly crystal stone beings you may have to access a store or website to find the right stones for you.

Many spiritual traditions tout the healing power of stones, minerals, and crystals. Since I was a little girl I talked to the rocks in my yard. To me, they were alive just like everything else. The reason I wanted to include crystals in a cookbook is because they can be part of powerful, healing teas and crystal infusions. You can actually drink your crystal healing!

Who I Am

Hi, I'm Amy and I have been proudly "woo woo" since I was a teenager! Here I am years later a bestselling author and internationally renowned medical intuitive. I was clairvoyant as a child and, as mentioned earlier, hung out with the stones and nature spirits in my yard. While I was in college getting a teaching degree I was also studying with many spiritual teachers, including a Native American-style medicine woman and several prominent medical intuitives. During that time I also became a Reiki Master Teacher.

For the last 15 years, I have been talking with people's spirit guides and traveling the world teaching different facets of everything I've learned on my ever evolving spiritual path. This book is another expression of my creative impetus to inspire and uplift my readers. I love you all!

Raising Vibrations

I feel like I am here on earth to promote living from the heart. To help us live from the heart and improve our health, as well as everything else in our lives we all need to raise our vibrations. In this case, vibration is the speed or frequency at which the matter and energy in our body vibrates. I have learned from my work as a medical intuitive that the easiest and most effective way to raise our vibrations is through the power of joy! So, what if we could bring the power of joy into our food and beverages? And, we could make them really colorful and surround them with sparkly beauty. That is my mission in this book. I want to teach you how to feed your chakras exactly what they need to empower your life. And I want you to have a blast with me while we power up your chakras!

How to Use This Book

In the coming chapters, I will take you on a journey through the basics of chakras and crystals and how they work together. Next, we will talk about crystal teas and infusions and how to make them. Then you will find the recipe section of the book where I share a juice recipe, a sorbet or smoothie recipe, a salad recipe, a crystal tea recipe, and affirmations to say while you make your delicious, colorful recipes for each chakra in the body. You can also look at the colors that are most resonating with you and start there.

But most of all have fun! I believe that food should be colorful, joyful, and spectacularly nourishing. Don't you?

Special Diets

Candida Diet - If you are on an anti-candida diet to prevent or treat candidiasis omit the more sugary fruits from the recipes and substitute stevia for the honey and maple syrup. Additionally, load up on oregano, thyme, clove, cinnamon, and lemon to suppress the Candida.

Alkaline Diet - Load up on lemon and lime - nature's alkalizers. Use less of the more sugary fruits like banana, mango, and pineapple that are more acidic. And try stevia in place of other sweeteners because stevia tastes sweet but contains zero sugar!

3

Vegan Diet - If you're vegan, this book is for you! You can substitute maple syrup or stevia for the honey mentioned.

Vegetarian Diet - Enjoy all this plant based goodness!

Gluten Free, Wheat Free Diet - Every recipe in this book is safe for you to enjoy.

Low Carbohydrate Diet - Emphasize the vegetables that are less starchy and the fruits with lower sugar, like berries and stone fruits.

If you have food allergies just make sure you read through everything and omit any ingredients that aren't for you. And everyone soak up the delicious, fiber filled light of every intentional recipe. No animals were harmed in the making of this book! May a compassionate world reign.

Share the Chakra and Crystal Love

I want to make sure that you have an amazing array of high vibrational, joyful options for your chakra crystal kitchen so I am going to be flooding my Instagram, Twitter, Snapchat, and Facebook (all @amyleighmercree) with gorgeous pictures and bonus recipes. And I want you all to meet each other! There is an awesome array of conscious people out there who believe plants and animals deserve respect and crystals are beings, too. So, let's all connect!

Share your creations from this cookbook and your own chakra or crystal recipes with the hashtag #chakrasandcrystalscookbook. I love talking with my readers!

4

CHAKRAS

If you're an athlete preparing for game day or a race, a bride-to-be going on a special diet, or one of the millions of people in the world with food allergies or intolerances, you already know that what you put into your body makes a huge difference in your daily life. Even if you don't relate to any of these scenarios you've certainly been in a situation where you over-indulged in something greasy, or turned to chicken soup or orange juice to fight a nasty cold. Chances are, you noticed pretty quickly that what you feed your body also nourishes your soul. Just like your body responds to specific foods, your chakras are engaged and empowered by the foods that you eat. Food is fuel that provides mental and physical energy, and when you need to achieve a particular goal, changing your diet to impact your chakras is a great way to start.

Here is a list of foods and flowers to turn to when you need specific chakra support. Remember to eat with intention: many foods on this list are good for your full chakra system, and some are specific to individual chakra needs.

Chakra	Flowers	Foods
Root Chakra	Bee balm, Dandelion, Red rose	Beets, turnips, protein-filled foods (meat, eggs, beans), red grapes, adzuki beans, beet greens, sage, oregano, thyme, cayenne pepper, cherries, cranberry, goji berry, pomegranate, black beans, ginger, parsnips, taro
Sacral Chakra	Calendula, Squash blossom, Gardenia	Mango, cantaloupe, seeds & nuts, pumpkin, wild salmon, sweet potato, persimmon, pappaya, figs, maple syrup, apple, apricot, peaches, nectarines, oranges, strawberry, brussels sprouts, carrots, butternut squash, acorn squash

Solar Plexus Chakra	Dill flower, Fennel, Melissa	Grains (pasta, cereal, rice), Complex carbohydrates (fiber, legumes), dairy products, lemons, fennel stalks, dill, starfruit, honey, banana, pineapple, artichoke, chickpeas, corn, chamomile, lemon grass, spaghetti squash, delicata squash
Heart Chakra	Cherry blossom, Broccoli, Cilantro, Jasmine, Lavender	Leafy greens, raw vegetables, comfort foods, broccoli, chard, green grapes, mint, cilantro, avocado, kiwi, lime, pear, arugula, mung beans, bean sprouts, peas, bok choy, celery, endive, parsley, lettuce, spinach, chives, scallions, zucchini, watercress
Throat Chakra	Borage, Nigella	Blueberries, blue potatoes, liquids (water, herbal teas, fruit juices), basil, boysenberry, red currant, watermelon

Third Eye Chakra	Angelica, Astello Indigo	Dark fruits, grape juice, caffeine, chocolate, blackberry, black currant
Crown Chakra	Campanula, Phlox, Violet, Lotus	Detoxifying foods, fresh air, cucumbers, dandelion greens, daikon radishes, wheatgrass, sprouts, plum, anise, lavender
Earth Star Chakra	Chamomile, Bougainvillea	Potatoes, garlic, plantain, cauliflower, cabbage, onion, shallots, leeks
Soul Star Chakra	Chervil, Pea blossom, Lemon verbana	Mushrooms, coconut, tropical fruits, passionfruit, lychee, water chestnut

Root Chakra

The root chakra is located at the base of your spine, and is associated with groundedness and protection. It impacts your feelings of security and stability. To balance the root chakra, eat the following:

Foods

Root vegetables, as their category implies, are grown underground, so they absorb a lot of nutrients from the soil. The vitamins, magnesium, potassium and other minerals found in many root vegetables can help you build stamina, prevent cancer, and regulate your immune system. Red root vegetables like beets and red potatoes are especially beneficial, as their rosy color shares vibrations with

10

your root chakra and will help diffuse stressful or negative energies associated with root chakra blockages. Turnips, parsnips and rutabagas are great veggies to turn to for your root chakra as well. Add them to salads, roast them, or eat them raw with a yummy dip!

Protein can be found in all sorts of foods, from tofu and soy products to nuts and beans. Protein strengthens your root chakra, while also fighting to prevent physical ailments like obesity and arthritis. It also improves your digestion, and keeps the rest of your body running smoothly. Your root chakra is the base of the chakra system. It's very important that it functions properly so everything else can fall into line. If you follow a vegetarian diet, make sure you are getting protein from sources like beans and nuts (or eggs, if you are not a vegan). Nourish your root chakra and keep yourself healthy, strong, and balanced.

Flowers

You'd never guess it from looking at them, but *Bee Balm* petals have a delicious, minty flavor. Also known as Bergamot, or Oswego Tea, this pretty red flower can be used to brew yummy teas, and is in fact what colonists used in America after protesting imported teas during the Boston Tea Party. Bee Balm helps fight off colds and fevers, and is also a good cure for insomnia. The lovely red color resonates with your root chakra, and adding blossoms to salads or desserts will leave you feeling strong and grounded.

Dandelion root is often seen as a weed—in fact, you may have recently pulled some from your flowerbeds—but you shouldn't underestimate its power to affect your root chakra. Dandelion is a detoxifier that will purge you of negative energies and release blockages in your kidneys and liver, which are both key root chakra organs. Add it to salads or cook it in the same way you would other leafy greens to keep your root chakra strong, and your spirit feeling balanced and secure.

Sacral Chakra

The sacral chakra is located in the lower abdomen, and is associated with creativity, sexuality, and reproduction. It opens you up to new experiences, and encourages you to explore new possibilities. To attend to your sacral chakra, eat the following:

Foods

Sweet fruits like cantaloupe, mango, strawberry, and oranges are great for opening and balancing your sacral chakra. Their juices will help stimulate your creativity and will leave you receptive to new methods and ideas. Try a fruit salad before embarking on major creative work, or a delicious fruit smoothie as a snack before date night. Remember, fruit is high in sugar, so be careful with your intake if you have insulin issues, or are indulging in other sweet treats at the same time.

Wild salmon is full of rich Omega-3's and healthy fats and oils, which share energetic vibrations with the sacral chakra. When eating for your sacral chakra, you want to look for foods that represent strength (protein) and flow (oils), so a salmon dish that incorporates hazelnuts or sesame seeds is an excellent choice. Extra points if you add a touch of orange, like citrus or carrots, to really get your sacral chakra spinning! (If you are vegan you can skip the salmon and pile on the sweet potatoes.)

Flowers

Calendula flower can taste spicy, tangy, or peppery—maybe that's why it's known in some culinary circles as "the poor man's saffron." Calendula is easy to grow yourself and tastes great when added to eggs, soups, or rice dishes.

When reduced to topical oils, they can even prevent or treat burns. The bright orange color of the calendula blossom, along with its medicinal value, stimulates the sacral chakra and promotes creative expression, so use it before date night, or when you are stuck on a tricky project.

Gardenia blossoms look a lot like jasmine flowers, so the two are often confused. They taste a lot like jasmine flowers too – flowery and sweet, a great reminder of your garden! Gardenias can be eaten raw, pickled, or preserved with honey, and will get your creativity flowing. Add a bouquet of gardenias to the bedroom, or use it to garnish a yummy dessert at the end of your romantic dinner to stimulate the sacral chakra and enhance your sense of fun.

Solar Plexus Chakra

The solar plexus chakra is located by your breastbone, and is associated with self-confidence and strength. It stimulates happiness and power, and when blocked can lead to being overly judgmental. To eat for the solar plexus chakra, consider the following:

Foods

Complex carbohydrates are found in whole grains and legumes, and includes plants like quinoa and brown rice. They are a great way to support the solar plexus chakra. Complex carbs help your digestive system, which adds vital energy to your body and mind. You can replace a lot of your usual carbohydrates with complex carbs by choosing brown instead of white rice in your burrito bowl, making steel cut oatmeal instead of the sweet instant kind, or replacing white flour pasta with quinoa. Don't shy away from bread with seeds and grains just because it looks less appetizing – those grains will do wonders for your overall happiness and self-confidence!

Flowers

Yellow *Dill flowers* taste a lot like dill leaves and have an excellent impact on your solar plexus chakra. The delicate yellow color inspires confidence and happiness. Add dill flowers to your pickle jar when pickling vegetables, toss them in chicken or tuna salad, or add them to your navy bean soup for extra flavor. It's also a good idea to have some dill before a run or heavy exercise, as feeding your solar plexus chakra builds strength end endurance.

Melissa, also known as lemon balm, is a lovely flower that cleanses your solar plexus chakra. It's known for regulating thyroid problems and gastrointestinal issues, and its oils can relax tense or strained muscles. The pretty yellow flowers are widely known to ease anxiety, and can help you focus on completing daily tasks with confidence. Sprinkle them onto fruit salads, make them into candy, or add them to your favorite baked goods.

Heart Chakra

The heart chakra is located in the center of your chest, and is associated with compassion and love. When it is open, the heart chakra allows you to express both self-love and love for others. To balance your heart chakra eat the following:

Foods

Leafy greens like arugula, lettuce, and kale not only display the rich green color that stimulates your heart chakra and promotes love and compassion, but are also full of heart-healthy nutrients. The little veins you see in your green leafy veggies represent the circulatory system, and are a nice model of the energy your heart chakra sends throughout your body. They're also rich in folic acid and vitamin K, which keep your body running smoothly, opening your heart chakra as you eat. Though healthiest when eaten raw in salads, leafy greens can be cooked into casseroles, steamed, or used in place of bread for wraps or rolls.

If you've ever turned to food to cheer you up after a bad break up or help you get through difficult news, you'll understand the nourishing value of *comfort foods*. In cold weather, many people choose soups or macaroni and cheese to mentally bring them back to a place of safety and security, often recollecting childhood and the feelings of love they remember from older relatives. To heal your heart chakra, unearth a childhood recipe and spread the most important ingredient—love—to yourself, your friends, and your family.

Flowers

The *cherry blossom* tree is a symbol of love and friendship. The soft color of its petals resonates with the vibrations of the secondary color of your heart chakra, pink. Cherry blossoms taste delicate and flowery, much like they smell, and can open your heart chakra and help you cultivate kindness and compassion. They are often used as decorations on cakes and pastries, and can be eaten along with any dessert. In Japan it is common to salt and pickle cherry blossoms and then add them to soups or teas for a dash of flavor and to inspire love.

Broccoli may show up on the menu as a vegetable, but those little florets at the top of your broccoli stems are actually flowers! Much like other green leafy veggies, broccoli's color is a symbol of its impact on the heart chakra, and of the nutrients inside of it that keep your physical body healthy. So now you know: all those times your parents told you to finish your broccoli, they really were insisting out of love! Eat broccoli raw with a yummy dip, or cook it into a stir-fry or pasta bake to open up compassion and love into your life.

Throat Chakra

The throat chakra is located at your neck, and is associated with clear communication and expression. An open throat chakra promotes honesty and the ability to feel safe speaking your mind. To balance your throat chakra eat the following:

Foods

Blueberries are a super food for more reasons than one! Full of fiber and antioxidants, these popular berries prevent heart disease, stimulate your brain health, and lower the cholesterol in your blood. They also encourage you to speak your mind and express your personal truth. When headed over to a friend's home to have a serious or difficult discussion, consider bringing a basket of fresh baked blueberry scones or muffins to ease the conversation along. On the morning of a big presentation, toss some blueberries into your yogurt or cereal to ensure that your talk goes smoothly. Both strategies will strengthen your communication abilities, and help you be more honest.

As you probably already know, there is nothing like a good cup of tea to soothe a sore throat. *Liquids* in general—fruit juices, teas, waters, even coffee—are great for opening your throat chakra and promoting honest communication. Sit down over a steaming cup of tea when telling a friend what's been on your mind, or when trying to be honest with yourself about a difficult decision. And make sure to always be drinking lots of water throughout your day so that your throat chakra is clear and your communication is open! Hydration is key to cleansing the throat chakra, and is great for your health in general.

Flowers

Borage is a pretty little blue flower that tastes slightly like cucumber. It is known for reducing congestion

16

and easing cough symptoms like swollen glands and sore throats. Add it as a garnish to drinks or salads, and notice how you find yourself more comfortable with speaking your mind. As your communication improves you'll also realize that those around you are more receptive to what you have to say. If your throat chakra is unbalanced, and you tend to talk too much and listen too little, borage can help you find balance in your communication styles. Add it to salads, or use it as a yummy edible garnish for lemonades and cocktails.

Nigella sativa is known for the amazing properties of its seeds—for thousands of years people have been using it to cure all sorts of ailments, including asthma, high blood pressure, epilepsy, and opiate withdrawals. It soothes hypertension and can help you feel relaxed and open to sharing your truths with others. Use it as a seasoning in place of cumin, or add a spoonful to smoothies or cereal.

Third Eye Chakra

The third eye chakra is located on your forehead above your eyebrows and is associated with spiritual awareness and psychic intuition. It helps you with creative problem solving, and when balanced will lower your stress levels. To balance your third eye chakra eat the following:

Foods

Grape juice is delicious. It also stimulates your third eye chakra and open you up to higher spiritual awareness. The dark indigo color of grape juice resonates with your third eye chakra colors and can help you approach problems in a new and creative way. Grape juices will also strengthen your natural physic intuitions and amplify any metaphysical signals you are experiencing.

Chocolate isn't just a decadent indulgence—it opens up your third eye chakra and strengthens your intuition and spiritual awareness. Dark chocolate especially is known for fighting inflammation and lowering blood pressure. Munch on some dark chocolate if you feel a headache coming on, or when you want to fine-tune your ability to interpret metaphysical messages. You can also have some chocolate (low sugar) before meditation to focus and clear your third eye.

Flowers

Angelica gets its name from, you guessed it, its association with angels. This lovely flower, which tastes a bit like celery, is great for opening your third eye chakra and helping you communicate metaphysically. All parts of the plant are edible, and are often found in stews or caramelized as a side dish. Angelica can also be candied and used as a garnish to any dessert. Combine candied angelica with chocolate cake to open your third eye and amplify messages from larger metaphysical energies.

Licorice Mint Hyssop is a pretty flower that comes in all the colors of the rainbow. Hyssop resonates with your third eye chakra and strengthens your intuition. It has a clean flavor that is perfect in salads, paired with pork, or stirred into tea or cocktails. Certain blossoms have a slight anise seed flavor, the main flavor in black licorice. Fans of licorice can nibble hyssop to get that specific taste while clearing their third eye chakra.

Crown Chakra

The crown chakra is located at the top of your head, and is associated with enlightenment and cosmic energy. A balanced crown chakra will lead to feelings of spiritual connection and well-being. To balance your crown chakra eat:

Foods

Cleansing foods are ideal for balancing your crown chakra. For centuries, numerous cultures have recommended short-term detoxifying diets as a way to enhance your spirituality and connect to cosmic energies. Detoxifying foods include cucumbers, dandelion greens, radishes, sprouts and especially wheatgrass juice. Consider detoxing by cutting out processed foods or chemicals to balance your crown chakra and keep your energies aligned.

Flowers

Campanula is commonly known as Bellflower, and its pretty purple color vibrates on the same frequency as your crown chakra energies. Adding campanula to your salads will help you feel a sense of spirituality. If growing your own, do some research and choose a strain that grows in your particular climate. While most spread like wildflowers, others can be trickier to cultivate.

Violet is the color of the crown chakra, so it stands to reason that violets are a great crown chakra food! Their petals and leaves can be eaten raw or cooked, or turned into syrup or jelly. They've been used to cure headaches and cure skin conditions, and some types have a divine fragrance. Add violets to your salads, or keep a big bouquet nearby when you sit down to practice yoga or to meditate. They will improve your practice and keep you spiritually open and aware.

Earth Star Chakra

The earth star chakra is located several feet below your feet, and is associated with earth energies and stability. It connects you to your soul's past incarnations, and creates a sense of being one with the earth. To take care of your earth star chakra eat:

Foods

The earth star chakra resonates with the colors black and brown, which means that *potatoes*, with their nutrient-filled skins, are the perfect food to nourish it. Just like your root chakra, the earth star chakra responds to root vegetables, which absorb numerous important vitamins and minerals as they grow in the ground. Make sure that your potato recipe includes the skins to both maximize your nutrition and stay in touch with your own roots.

Garlic adds a kick to any recipe, but the magic of those spicy little bulbs will also boost your physical health. It lowers your blood pressure, leaving you calm and grounded, and helps fight everything from the common cold to menstrual cramps. By strengthening your immune system, garlic builds up your defenses, stabilizing your mental and spiritual energies and helping cleanse and balance your earth star chakra.

Flowers

The beautiful *Bougainvillea* has been used for respiratory ailments for centuries, and can be taken to fight symptoms of asthma, flus and colds. It is also known as a "transition" flower, and can help ease the stress and tension of new experiences, whether it's starting a new job, moving, or embarking on a new romantic relationship. By stimulating your earth chakra, bougainvillea will help you feel secure in yourself and your spiritual journey before you embark on your new adventure. Bougainvillea blossoms pair well with arugula in salads, and can also be added to lemonades or teas.

Chamomile tea has a long history of soothing nerves and stomachs, but its dried flowers can also be added to cookies or breads, and is delicious when infused into ice creams! Chamomile activates all of your chakras, but is especially good for your earth star chakra. It will make you feel relaxed and centered, balancing your chakra system and preparing you for the day's challenges.

Soul Star Chakra

The soul star chakra is located several feet above your head, and is associated with spiritual growth and enlightenment. It connects you to the larger metaphysical universe, and leaves you open to communication from higher powers and forces.

Foods

Mushrooms support the soul star chakra because their white color opens the chakra and clears out all negative energies. In popular culture, mushrooms have often been associated with metaphysical communication and exploration of higher consciousness, whether they be the normal kind you find at the grocery store, or the kind Alice finds on her adventures in Wonderland! Adding mushrooms to a salad or a well-cooked portobello burger is a great way to support your soul star chakra and enhance your spirituality.

Not only are they juicy and delicious, but *tropical fruits* such as mangos, passion fruit, coconut, and papaya can activate your soul star chakra and put you in touch with higher energies and powers. Often associated with the sacral chakra, these fruits promote creativity and growth, opening you up to new ideas and thought processes. A tropical fruit smoothie or snack before meditation can enhance your spiritual awareness, and leave you receptive to higher energies and powers.

Flowers

Pea blossoms are exactly what they sound like: the pale flowers that bloom before your garden pea crop comes in. They taste faintly like peas themselves, but with

21

the added bonus that they cleanse and clear your soul star chakra and invoke higher energies and spirits. Just be careful not to confuse your pea blossoms with flowering ornamental sweet peas, which are toxic!

Lemon verbena is sometimes known as lemon bee-brush. It gives off a yummy lemony scent, and adds a bright citrus flavor to your cooking. These soft leaves and little white flowers can help reduce digestive issues, boost your immune system, strengthen your muscles, aid in weight loss, and calm your nerves. They also activate your soul star chakra and enhance your connection to higher metaphysical concepts and spirits.

"Your chakras are pools of energy filled from rivers of vibration coursing through your body."
Amy Leigh Mercree
#chakrasandcrystals cookbook

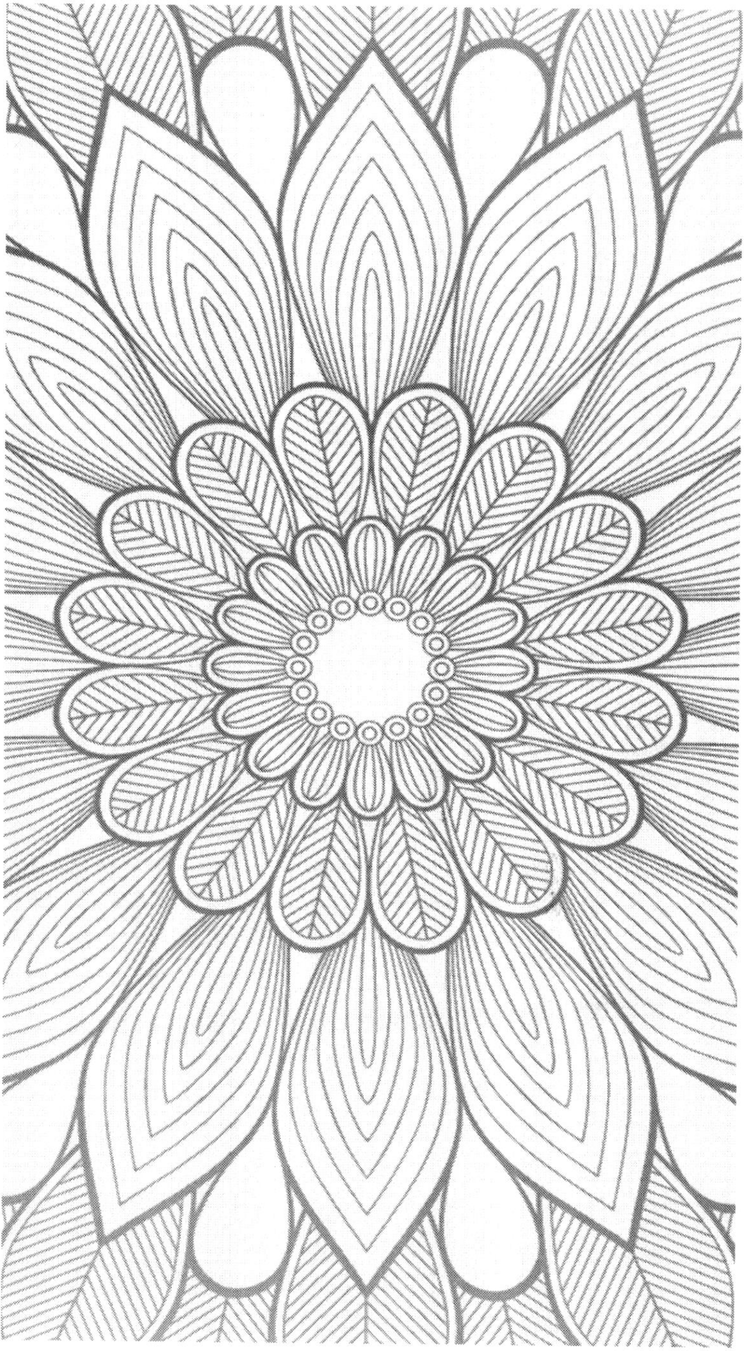

CRYSTAL HEALING
101

So your therapist or friend has recommended you use crystals to recalibrate your emotions, promote physical well-being, or focus your meditation. You've ordered some beautiful gemstones online, or found your favorites at a local boutique or your yard, and brought them into your home to begin the healing process. But what now? How does crystal therapy work, and how can you use it most effectively?

Crystal therapy has been a popular healing technique for thousands of years, and can be found in Ancient Egyptian, Greek, and Mayan traditions. Today's crystal healing is mostly based on concepts borrowed from Asian cultures: the Chinese idea of chi (life-energy), and the Buddhist and Hindu concept of chakras. Chakras, those spinning energy centers found throughout your body that keep your spiritual and physical health in line, can be opened or closed to restore balance in your life. Each individual chakra responds to a different type of crystal, hence the vast array of healing gemstones and geodes available.

Crystals are physical bodies comprised of energy, but like any other physical object, they also have a spiritual aura. If you've ever heard someone talking about subtle bodies, they are probably referring to the metaphysical energies that crystals and geodes emit. Each particular crystal has its own inherent metaphysical harmony that works something like a tuning fork, balancing any distorted patterns that it encounters and helping various energies in the human body to work together. Imagine Woolly Willy, that kids' toy from the 1950s that let you use a magnetic pen to move bits of magnetic dust around to create facial hair patterns. Healing crystals work much like that magnetic pen, but instead of dust, they are creating patterns out of energy.

Just looking at structures of gemstones, you can get a sense for their adherence to patterns. When you see the shimmering, geometric facets of crystals and gemstones, it's hard not to consider the greater hand that was involved in creating such delicate configurations. Each crystal's pattern holds a small electrical charge that resonates with different aspects of your own energies, and can thus be used to bring your chakras or chi back in line. If you pay attention, you'll see crystal vibrations impacting other objects you use everyday: liquid crystal diodes are used in calculators and computers, and can also be found in laser technology and fiber-optics.

Because each crystal's pattern is unique, different stones have their own values and properties. For example, azurite is known for its ability to awaken psychic abilities and point you toward spiritual guidance, which means it's a good choice for someone who needs to attend to her Third Eye or Crown Chakras. Carnelian, a smooth, swirled, orange stone, is attuned to the Sacral Chakra, and promotes courage, compassion, and creativity. Jade has long been known to bring luck, and Rose Quartz is associated with self-compassion and forgiveness. Even common gemstones found in jewelry stores, like turquoise and fresh-water pearls, have their own particular resonance and can be used purposefully for their healing properties.

There are several methods by which you can use crystal healing at home. The simplest and most common way to use crystals is to wear them on or near your body. Without realizing it, you may have already intuitively selected jewelry with gems that your body needs. For example, that turquoise bracelet you always wear is more than just a gorgeous accessory: it promotes honest communication, and works to strengthen and align all of the chakras. If you have a specific problem you need to deal with, choose a crystal that is known for its effect on the associated chakras. Though you don't need to place the crystal directly on the area related to your treatment, it is certainly beneficial to do so. If you are wearing a crystal pendant, pay attention to the length of your chain: if you are trying to focus on your Throat Chakra, keep it shorter, and let it hang down onto your chest if you want to direct energies to your Heart Chakra.

Using crystals for cleansing is also very common. You can place crystals by your bath to absorb any stresses and negative energies as you rinse and relax. You can also put crystals in specific areas of your office or home if you feel the need to neutralize stressful or bad energies. Raw crystals are most useful for this, as they require less cleansing between uses. Hang them on your balcony or porch to absorb environmental pollution and city noise.

For major goals and affirmations, consider building your own crystal grid. A crystal grid combines the energies of multiple crystals and magnifies their power. Select crystals are placed in a specific geometric shape, and the synergy of the specially chosen crystals and the intricate shape works toward a particular, defined goal. To set up your crystal grid, you'll need an open, cleansed space, a selection of crystals, and a clearly defined goal. If you are a beginner, it also helps to have a grid layout, which you can find in stores, or print out at home. Intention is key when creating your crystal grid: write down your goal, and make sure you are as specific as possible. Then choose stones that resonate with the goal you've chosen. As you set up your crystal grid, keep your goal or intention firmly in your mind, even stating it out loud if your intuition guides you to do so. Once the pattern is set, use a quartz crystal point to draw lines between the stones, which will connect all of their energies. Try to set the grid up in a space you are in often, but that won't need to be tidied up anytime soon. Crystal grids are most effective if you leave them set up for at least two months!

Finally, a great way to use crystal healing is during meditation. Again, you will need to choose crystals that resonate with the particular goals or intentions you have when meditating: if you are trying to relieve stress, pick something like amethyst or chrysocolla; if you are focused on becoming a better communicator, select blue lace agate or sodalite. Once you've selected the best crystal for your purpose, conduct your meditation practice as you usually would, with the crystal nearby or in your hand. This will enhance the usual benefits of both the crystal and your meditation.

Because there are so many varieties of crystals and gemstones, it may take a bit of research before you find the perfect match for your specific therapeutic needs. Luckily, there are all kinds of resources online and at your local library or boutique that can help you find the perfect crystal for your purpose and help you make the most of crystal therapy!

Asking Permission

Guess what? Crystals are living beings! Just like a plant, animal or person, a crystal has an oversoul and awareness of what's happening to it and its surroundings. It's very important that we always ask a crystal's permission before we move it or use it for something or put it in our crystal infusion tea.

To ask a crystal what it would like to do or if it is consenting to being moved or placed on a chakra or put near a tea infusion you can use the following process:

"*Stones & crystals are alive & deserve care & respect.*"
Amy Leigh Mercree
#chakrasandcrystals
cookbook

Crystal Connection Meditation

Pick up or hover your hands over the rock, stone, or crystal with which you'd like to connect. Close your eyes and bring your awareness to the palms of your hands. Notice any sensation there such as pulsing or tingling. This is you and the stone exchanging energy. Now say the following invocation aloud, "I ask to communicate with the crystal and stone people for the very highest good of all life. I choose to help all and harm none."

With your eyes still closed, focus your attention on the crystal or stone that you would like to talk to, and with your mind or out loud say the word hello.

Pause, and listen with your heart and your spirit for the stone being to answer back. After you feel that part of the exchange is complete then you can tell the crystal anything else you would like.

Next, ask the crystal the specific question you're inquiring about. It might be, "May I place you next to my cup of warm water and herbs to infuse your essence in the water so I may drink it?" Or it might be something like, "May I place you on my heart chakra to help me open and clear it?"

If the crystal says no do not be offended. It's just like if someone asked you, "Can I pick you up and put you in the middle of a heavy metal concert?" If you're not a fan of heavy metal you might say no. Conversely, in many instances, it might be like if someone asked to pick you up and put you in the middle of a relaxing yoga class. You might like that. So you'd say yes to that.

Ask your crystal what would be the best place for it to be? Would it like a sea salt bath in a bowl of its choosing? Would it like to be placed in cool water? Would it like to be on a sunny windowsill for a few days? Does it need a moon bath and would like to be outside in your grass on the full moon this month? Would it prefer to be placed in the bowl of sand? Is it ready to retire and it wants you to hike it out into the middle of the woods and leave it there or gently place it in the ocean?

Once you've completed all of that communication you can thank the crystal and have any more conversation or exchange that you would like and then when you're done you can place the crystal back on the table or rug and state aloud, "I lovingly disconnect from this stone as needed for my highest good, the stone's highest good, and the highest good of all life."

Chakra	Herbs	Crystals & Gemstones
Root Chakra	Dandelion root, Elderberry flower, Astragalus root, Wild lettuce leaf	Hematite, Black Obsidian, Garnet, Smoky Quartz
Sacral Chakra	Damiana, Maca, Calendula, Pine, Vervain	Vanadinite, Carnelian, Orange Calcite, Crocoite
Solar Plexus Chakra	Rosemary, Marshmallow leaf, Fenugreek, Star Anise	Citrine, Yellow Sapphire, Gold, Amber, Sunstone
Heart Chakra	Hawthorn berry, Green tea, Jasmine, Yerba Santa	Rose Quartz, Malachite, Jade, Aventurine
Throat Chakra	Red clover blossom, Lemongrass, Licorice, Comfrey	Blue Lace Agate, Lapis Lazuli, Larimar, Angelite
Third Eye Chakra	Feverfew, Eyebright, Valerian root, Gingko	Charoite, Sugilite, Violet Fluorite, Labradorite
Crown Chakra	Lavender, Frankincense, Comfrey, Mugwort	Amethyst, Clear Quartz, Diamond, Howlite
Earth Star Chakra	Burdock, Wintergreen, Cat's Claw bark	Gray Agate, Chiastolite, Dravite

Soul Star Chakra	Angelica, Sweet-grass, St. John's wort	Rainbow Quartz, Selenite, Moonstone, Phenakite
Hand Chakra	Ginger, Pepper-mint	Clear & Smokey Quartz, Moldavite
Foot Chakra	Passionflower, Virginia Bluebells	Dalmatian Jasper, Blue Kyanite, Tourmaline

When doing energy work and realigning your chakras, specific herbs and crystals can provide guidance and assistance. It's commonly known that herbs have strong medicinal qualities, but, just like crystals, they also emit specific vibrations that can help balance your chakras and keep your mental and physical health in line. Herbal and crystal energies can help you with personal growth, and by selecting the appropriate crystals and herbs, you can promote positivity and power in your life. Take a look at this list of chakras, and their associated herbs and crystals, to ensure that your chakras are balanced and your energies are clear.

Root Chakra

The root chakra is located at the base of your spine, and is associated with groundedness and stability. To balance the root chakra use:

Crystals/Gemstones

Hematite is a beautiful, smooth stone that grounds and protects you, making it perfect for the root chakra. It supports your nervous system and improves your memory, helping you feel centered and connected as you go about your day. Hematite also helps you keep your thoughts in order, so it is great to turn to when you feel overwhelmed by your to-do list.

Obsidian, formed when lava cools and hardens into shiny black stones, is known for its uses as a "guardian stone" that protects you both physically and metaphysically from negative energies. It contains many earthly properties that will resonate with the root chakra and leave you feeling confident and strong. Obsidian has many physical benefits, including fighting viral infections and improving the health of your stomach and muscle tissue.

Herbs

Dandelion is a great herb for the root chakra, as it is an adaptogen, which means it stabilizes your body's physiological processes. Herbs in this class help you physically adapt to all kinds of stressors, including temperature extremes, loud noises, changes in altitude, and changing schedules. They promote endurance and strength, so they are an ideal choice for when you want to ground yourself by balancing your root chakra. Other adaptogens that you can add to food or brew into teas include *Holy Basil, Ginseng*, and *Rhodiola rosea*.

Dried *Elderberry flower* has been an ingredient in restorative teas for centuries. It calms a busy mind, leaving you feeling centered and grounded after a stressful or busy day. If you are making your own elderflower tea, be careful! While the flowers have amazing healing properties, elderflower bark contains toxic chemicals, so avoid them when gathering and brewing.

Sacral Chakra

The sacral chakra is located below your stomach between the belly button and reproductive organs, and is associated with creativity, sexuality, and reproduction. When the sacral chakra is open and flowing, it opens you up to new experiences and encourages you to explore new possibilities. To balance the sacral chakra use:

Crystals/Gemstones

Carnelian, with its lovely orange glow, is well-known to stimulate the sacral chakra and provide bursts of creative thought and feeling. It helps with motivation, and attracts prosperity and luck to those who carry it! Its name comes from the Latin word for flesh, so needless to say it can also inspire creativity in the bedroom. Place some carnelian by your desk or on your nightstand to open your sacral chakra and promote all types of creative thought and action.

Orange calcite is a mood booster that interacts with your sacral chakra to alleviate depression and self-doubts. It also helps balance your reproductive system and relieve intestinal troubles. Orange calcite is great for a needed boost of sexual energy, and can enhance a romantic evening by getting your sacral chakra spinning.

Herbs

Not only are *Calendula* flowers bright orange, when added to tea they both promote creativity, and boost your circulation. Calendula is also known to ease menstrual cramps and pains, ovarian cysts, and symptoms of menopause. This makes dried calendula the perfect herb for the sacral chakra, which controls your sexuality and reproductive drive.

Often, our sexual freedom is blocked because we feel ashamed of our bodies' natural desires. A tea made from *pine needles* is just the thing to help cleanse you of any blame or regret you feel toward your own sexuality. Pine is often recommended for men who need a boost of testosterone, so a bit of pine's healing essence is ideal just before a romantic date night at home!

Solar Plexus Chakra

The solar plexus chakra is located by your breast-bone, and is associated with self-confidence and strength. It stimulates happiness and power, and when blocked can lead to being overly judgmental. To balance the solar plexus chakra use:

Crystals/Gemstones

Often called the stone of abundance, *citrine* is a wonderful choice of stone to heal your solar plexus chakra and increase your self-esteem. It promotes success and mental clarity, and can magnify your personal power and energy. Citrine fights against negative energies, so it is a great choice to use when you set up a crystal grid or want to cleanse your home or work environment. It clears negative energies without absorbing them, so you can leave it up for months or even years without having to do regular energy cleansings, making it perfect for those with limited free time.

Amber has a calming energy that will simultaneously both settle your mind and infuse you with confident energies. It is considered a good luck charm, and brings patience and protection to those who use it. Amber will purify your mind and body, so it is great for flushing negative thoughts and building your self-esteem and confidence.

Herbs

Marshmallow leaf is best known for its initial involvement in the manufacturing of marshmallows, but as an herb makes a soothing, comforting tea that balances your solar plexus chakra. It helps with digestion, and reconnects you to your breath, helping you relax and embrace your natural confidence.

Rosemary is another must-have herb for the solar

plexus chakra. You can add it to your food, use rosemary oil, or brew a yummy tea to sooth any stomach pains and clear your intestinal tract. Rosemary will increase your vitality and strengthen your health, leaving you ready to handle any difficulties you encounter throughout the day.

Heart Chakra

The heart chakra is located in the center of your chest, and is associated with compassion and love. When it is open, the heart chakra allows for you to express both self-love, and love for others. To balance the heart chakra use:

Crystals/Gemstones

Known as the love stone, *rose quartz* opens your heart chakra and encourages unconditional love. It is a high-energy crystal, and can enhance love and compassion in a variety of situations. Use rose quartz when you need a boost of self-love, or as a gift for someone who you want to make sure recognizes the love you are feeling for them. Rose quartz is beautiful in jewelry, so it makes a great necklace that you can rest over your heart chakra to increase its effect.

Malachite is a gorgeous green stone that represents pure love and protection. It is a stone of transformation, and will help with your spiritual evolution by releasing energy blockages and encouraging growth. Malachite is a great stone to use as you try to rid yourself of unhealthy relationships, as it encourages positive, healthy love that clears your heart chakra and shows you the type of love that you deserve.

Herbs

Hawthorn berries strengthen your heart and your blood vessels. These delicious red fruits improve circulation, but also heal at a metaphysical level. Hawthorn berries clear emotional blockages as they assist your heart physically, opening you up to experience joy and gratitude. Hawthorn is also known to help begin the healing process if you feel your heart has been broken, so it is a great choice to bring to a friend getting over a breakup, or to take yourself when experiencing great loss.

If your heart chakra is blocked, *green tea* can help you cleanse and clear it. It will reduce your risk of heart disease by increasing antioxidants in your blood, clearing negative energies and paving the way for an open, balanced heart chakra. Though many green teas don't have a strong green color, it is enough to connect with your heart chakra and get your energy flowing!

Throat Chakra

The throat chakra is located at your neck, and is associated with clear communication and expression. An open throat chakra promotes honesty and the ability to feel safe speaking your mind. To balance the throat chakra use:

Crystals/Gemstones

Blue lace agate is a harmonious stone that enhances your intuition, and brings you confidence in your own voice. Associated with tact and clearness of expression, blue lace agate can help calm your nerves before a large public speaking engagement, ease the flow of a difficult conversation, and even assist with speech impediments and nervous vocal tics. It is a hopeful stone that encourages happiness and tranquility, so it is a great choice for those looking to balance their throat chakras.

For a long time, *lapis lazuli* was known for its rarity, and was used to create the lovely royal blue color you see in older paintings. Today, it is said to promote truthful communication. If you are struggling with how to make a point, or how to kindly and tactfully tell your coworker or partner something you know they won't want to hear, lapis lazuli can help you find just the right words to do so. It brings you spiritual love and hope, and resonates strongly with your throat chakra.

Herbs

Your throat chakra is the control center of your communicative abilities, and *Red clover blossom* is known for unleashing emotions and helping you find words for how you are feeling. Share a cup of red clover blossom tea with a friend or loved one during a difficult conversation and notice how open you feel toward them. You can find red clover blossom all over – just look around for those purple clover flowers you see in backyards or forests.

Lemongrass is an excellent remedy for a sore throat. It reduces inflammation and, as an herb of peace and healing, diffuses anger, tension, and conflict. Use it before public speaking, or to calm down an escalating argument with a family member or friend. Lemongrass is also a great addition to soups, or to help soothe you as either a bath oil or candle during a relaxing soak in the tub.

Third Eye Chakra

The third eye chakra is located on your forehead, above your eyebrows and is associated with spiritual awareness and psychic intuition. It helps you with creative problem solving, and when balanced will lower your stress levels. To balance the third eye chakra use:

Crystals/Gemstones

Charoite is a stone generally used for prophesy and clairvoyance, so it stands to reason that it resonates strongly with your third eye chakra. It is an inspirational stone that transforms negative energies to positive ones, and can speed up healing energies of both the mental and physical variety. Charoite is a stone of creativity, and can often show you previously unsought paths to take and new ways to solve pressing problems. Use it when you feel stuck or blocked creatively.

Sugilite enhances healing, and amplifies psychic and spiritual abilities. Use it when channeling spirits or energies, or when you need an extra bit of psychic or spiritual protection. If you have natural telepathic or psychic gifts, sugilite will enhance them. A glimmering purple stone, sugilite will give you a feeling of freedom as it lowers your inhibitions and dispels your anger and tension. You can also use it to relieve headaches and other upper body discomfort.

Herbs

What better herb than eyebright to literally brighten your third eye and intuition? Eyebright is used for visual maladies, and also clarifies and enhances your perception. It's used to help with memory, and can open up your third eye chakra and make you more spiritually alert. It makes a great incense, or can be brewed into a sweet, delicious tea.

Feverfew helps clear emotional blockages that keep you from being open to new ideas. It calms you, boosts your spirits, and leaves you receptive to spiritual awareness and a greater world view. As its name implies, in the past it was often used to heal fevers and pains, and is still used today to enhance mental clarity and throw off sickness.

Crown Chakra

The crown chakra is located at the top of your head, and is associated with enlightenment and cosmic energy. A balanced crown chakra will lead to feelings of spiritual connection and well being. To balance the crown
39

chakra use:

Crystals/Gemstones

Amethyst is a stone well known for its deep purple color and lovely sparkle. You'll often find it in jewelry, but it is more than just a decorative gem. Amethyst promotes inner peace, and balances your psychic and physical energies. It brings inner strength and opens you up to spiritual insight. Amethyst is also known for its powers in helping with sobriety, so use it when you are trying to rid yourself of addictive behaviors.

Diamond, the hardest crystal, and one of the most expensive, helps you tap into the divine energy of the universe. It has very high frequency energy, and opens you up to spiritual awareness, stimulating your crown chakra and increasing your psychic intuition. Diamonds can help you with telepathic communication, and are great stones to use in mediation or for spiritual insight. Diamonds are also known for their ability to amplify the healing powers of all stones they come in contact with, so use them to give an extra boost to not only your crown chakra, but any other chakras you are hoping to balance or clear.

Herbs

Lavender is an herb often used to enhance meditation, so it stands to reason that it can assist in opening your crown chakra and getting you ready to accept divine inspiration and wisdom. It's more commonly found in essential oils, but a lavender tea can help you relax and enter a metaphysical state of mind. Lavender is also delicious in cocktails – keep an eye out for it on the menu at your favorite spot to grab an after work drink!

Countless cultures have used *frankincense* to aid in meditation, purification and other activities related to the crown chakra for thousands of years. Frankincense targets areas of your brain that help you feel more open and able to connect with greater concepts and spirits. It is a great spiritual cleanser, and will make you more receptive to metaphysical forces and the positive influence of the greater universe.

Earth Star Chakra

The earth star chakra is located several feet below your feet, and is associated with earthly energies and stability. It connects you to your soul's past incarnations, and creates a sense of being one with the earth. To balance the earth star chakra use:

Crystals/Gemstones

Dravite is a form of brown tourmaline that possesses protective energies. It combats anxiety and stresses, helping you feel stable and relaxed in difficult situations. Dravite is known for its role as a protector of the home, which makes it the ideal earth star chakra stone, connecting you to your home on earth and keeping you grounded and centered. Use it when you feel unstable, or to initiate a new home or office after a major move.

Chiastolite is known as a stone of harmony and balance. Metaphysically, chiastolite enhances astral travel and projection, giving you a solid grounding as your spirit explores outside of your body. It is also used to prevent or fight off high blood pressure, blood circulation problems, and rheumatism. Chiastolite will help you with creative problem solving, giving you multiple angles from which to view a sticky situation, and opening you up to new ideas.

Herbs

Full of calcium, nutrients, and anti-fungal properties, *burdock root* can reconnect you to the earth's energy. Its roots, leaves and seeds can all be used to balance and stimulate your earth star chakra and increase your connection to nature by promoting groundedness and stability. Since it is so full of nutrition, burdock root will help your physical body feel strong as it cleanses and clears your mental energy.

When in the ground, *wintergreen* absorbs and retains energies from the earth that can help you feel centered and balanced. Use it when you need to remind yourself about the beauty of nature and the world, or when the busy pace of modern life is too overwhelming.

Soul Star Chakra

The soul star chakra is located several feet above your head, and is associated with spiritual growth and enlightenment. It connects you to the larger metaphysical universe, and leaves you open to communication from higher powers and forces. To balance the soul star chakra use:

Crystals/Gemstones

Also known as *Desert Rose, selenite* is a transparent stone that comes from the Greek word for moon. It is a stone of mental clarity, enhancing your mental flexibility and accessing the energy of your subconscious mind. Many people use selenite to contact and communicate with angels or spirit guides. It removes energy blocks, so it is a great stone to use to heighten the effects of other stones, or to center your crystal grid. It is also a very soft stone, so can be molded or carved very easily to suit your purposes.

Phenakite is an extraordinarily high-energy crystal that is often used during meditation. It can cleanse and activate all of your chakras, but is especially associated with the soul star chakra, as it can help you to make contact with higher beings and metaphysical powers. People are often surprised at how powerful phenakite can be, so be ready for a burst of power before you use it for crystal healing.

Herbs

Angelica, as its name would suggest, has long been associated with angels. It can be used to protect against negative influences, and is known for opening you up to greater spiritual awareness. Though angelica is a fabulous herb, it is not ideal for all situations. If you are pregnant, be careful to avoid angelica, as it can have long-term effects on gestation and the health of your pregnancy and your child.

Sweetgrass is an ideal herb for the Soul Star chakra, as it attracts benevolent energies and spirit guides, helping you become more receptive to the messages they have to give you. Use it in incense or as an essential oil, or brew a tea to clear your mind and open yourself to higher light energies and powers.

Hand Chakra

The hand chakras are located in your palms and fingers, and are associated with giving and receiving energy. Blocked hand chakras are often associated with creative blocks and difficulty making connections with other people. To balance the hand chakra use:

Crystals/Gemstones

Moldavite is a powerful, high-energy stone that strengthens your own vibrational level as you use it. It will channel and heighten your own inner energies, allowing you to share energy with others. Moldavite is also associated with channeling, which means it will help you open yourself up to other energies outside of yourself and make the best use of them.

43

Smokey Quartz is a grounding stone that is often associated with the root chakra, but stimulates the hand chakras as well. It promotes cooperation and companionship, helping group efforts manifest with its unique energy. If you are having trouble working in a group setting, smokey quartz can help you reach your goals by diffusing negative energies and bringing all of the participants in your project together.

Herbs

Ginger warms you and improves your circulation, so it is perfect to kick-start your hand chakras and get your energy flowing. Drink ginger tea before working on a hands-on artistic project, or before you embark on a healing task with a partner. You will feel your blood pumping and your energies tingling in your hands as you work!

Peppermint builds your confidence, which means that after a cup of peppermint tea you can comfortably trust in your own intuition. Shake hands with a new friend or acquaintance and notice how your palms respond. The peppermint's effect on your hands will be a clue as to how you should relate to this person moving forward.

Foot Chakra

The foot chakras are located in your feet and toes, and are associated with communication and connection to the earth. Balanced foot chakras allow you to, as the saying goes, "walk the walk", rather than just "talking the talk." To balance the foot chakra use:

Crystals/Gemstones

Dalmatian jasper, sometimes called dalmatine, protects users from nightmares and negative thoughts. If you have trouble letting go and living in the moment, it can help you let loose and have some fun, by grounding you in the present moment. It's also a great stone for relationship building, as it promotes loyalty and helps you see multiple sides of a situation.

Blue kyanite is another stone that increases loyalty, which is perfect for your foot chakras. Often, people with blocked foot chakras have trouble with commitment. Kyanite, with its ability to encourage channeling, will help you stick to your plans and put the effort in to achieve your goals. Blue kyanite removes energy blockages, improves meditation practice, and works to align and balance all of your chakras together.

Herbs

Passionflower is a delicious smelling, calming herb that helps settle your nerves and focus on the task at hand. When your foot chakras are unbalanced, you often have trouble following through with goals and activities. Passionflower will motivate you and get you moving so that you can accomplish everything on your to-do list!

Lastly, the essence of *Virginia bluebells* will dispel any fears you have that are blocking your foot chakras. It has great healing powers and can lift your spirits on a dull or difficult day, opening you up to both divine and earthly energies.

"Crystals
are living beings
who can become friends
& healers if you treat
them with care."
Amy Leigh Mercree
#chakrasandcrystals
cookbook

RADIANT RECIPES

I have created an array of radiant recipes for you to use to empower each of your chakras! To decide which recipe to make, you can read about the chakras in the earlier chapters and see which one you would like to boost for the day. Or you can use of the ancient art of bibliomancy and open the book to a random page and whichever recipe you land on make that.

You may notice that you are drawn to certain colors and you might choose to make a recipe that goes with the corresponding chakra. You can think about what's going on in your life and what qualities would help you to manifest your dreams. For example, you might need some creativity for a project and then you could choose one of our second chakra recipes. Or, you might want to see a situation in your life more clearly and then you choose one of our sixth chakra recipes. The possibilities are endless.

Choose Organic
Your Health

Although many conventional farming funded food studies will disagree, the fact is nutritional value of fruits and vegetables begins to drop almost immediately after being harvested. One example is fresh broccoli. It loses as much as 50% of its vitamin C content seven days after being harvested. The rise of genetically modified food is making this problem even worse. Organically grown foods are usually consumed locally or more quickly than conventionally grown produce. Conventionally grown produce can sit on the shelf for weeks and spend longer periods of time being transported. So the nutritional value of the produce is continually dropping during that entire time.

If a fruit, vegetable or food product is 100% organic that means that it was not sprayed with any pesticides. And it is not genetically modified. Many pesticides have been proven to be carcinogenic including: organochlorines, creosote, and sulfallate. Organochlorines DDT, chlordane, and lindane are proven to promote tumors. Other studies show that contaminants contained in commercial pesticides are carcinogenic. Arsenic compounds and insecticides used regularly in commercial farming have been classified as carcinogenic by the International Agency for Research on Cancer.

Carcinogens are compounds that are proven to cause cancer. One carcinogen you may have heard of is cigarette smoke. For many years people believed cigarette smoking was safe and encouraged it. Even pregnant women were completely in the clear to smoke. Now we know how dangerous cigarette smoking is and that it's proven to cause cancer along with many other health problems. I believe the fight for our food is the fight for our health. And it's analogous to being exposed to carcinogens like cigarette smoke. The more we are able to eat organic food I believe the more healthy we will be. What do you think? Let me know on any of my social channels at #chakrasandcrystalscookbook.

The Planet's Health

You have the power to affect environmental change on our planet by choosing to purchase organic fruits, vegetables, and foods. You can be a force in preventing soil and underground water contamination caused by conventional farming which uses large quantities of artificial fertilizers and pesticides.

Organic farming is best for local wildlife. By not poisoning the natural habitat for plants and animals through forgoing toxic chemicals a kinder and less impactful farmer reduces the harm caused to local flora and fauna. Organic farming also helps fight global warming and encourages biodiversity. Biodiversity encourages the natural balancing of nature and keeps more species of plants and animals happy and healthy. It is the way mother nature intended flora and fauna to live together. And we are fauna. We are animals. Human animals. We have the opportunity to make a positive difference on our planet by choosing to put our money into causes we believe in. We vote with our dollars. And by purchasing organic foods we vote for a kinder and gentler planet.

"Buying organic
is the kind choice. Less
habitat loss for animals.
Less pollution."
Amy Leigh Mercree
#chakrasandcrystals
cookbook

JUICING FOR HEALTH

Juicing is an incredible way to deliver a boost of energy and a burst of vitamins to your body. When you use a juicer you remove the fiber from the juice of the fruit or vegetables that you are using for your recipe. By doing that you deliver a more easily digestible form of vitamins minerals and live raw enzymes to your body. When the fiber is included in the juice in something like a smoothie your body has to work a little bit harder to extract the nutrients from it. When you deliver it in a fresh juice form it's almost like taking a liquid vitamin because your body is able to absorb it early on in your digestive tract.

You may have heard of leaky gut syndrome which is basically increased permeability in different portions of our intestinal systems. When someone has leaky gut syndrome it means that they are losing a portion of the nutrients in their foods because they are leaking through the walls of their intestines and into the rest of the body. And they may also be leaking toxic substances, that are meant to be eliminated via digestion, into their bloodstream. As a result, people who may have some degree of leaky gut syndrome do well with liquid vitamins and fresh juices because more of those nutrients can be absorbed earlier in the digestive tract before they reach the areas of the intestines that are prone to leaking.

Many people conjecture leaky gut is caused by pesticides we ingest and other environmental toxins. The result of leaky gut is also diminished intestinal flora. With that we often also see diminished production of digestive enzymes from our stomach, pancreas, gallbladder, and liver. When we drink freshly juiced vegetables and fruits we deliver vital nutrients to our digestive system in a form that is more easily broken down.

To get the most nutritional value from your juice chew it a little bit. How do you chew a liquid you might wonder? That sounds silly! It actually stimulates the digestive enzymes that are excreted via your salivary glands and so by chewing your juice a little bit you begin the digestive process in your mouth and esophagus then when your juice get down into the early part of your stomach it is ready to be absorbed giving you a flash of micro-nutrients and enzymes that your body desperately needs.

"Drinking fresh juice provides a blissful burst of vital nutrients & vitamins." Amy Leigh Mercree #chakrasandcrystals cookbook

Juicers and the Mechanics of Juicing

There are two main types of juicers: centrifugal juicers and press juicers. If you do not already have a juicer and are looking to purchase one do some research on the topic. Different people have different opinions on which type of juicer is better. I will share my opinion with you here and it is coming from a more practical standpoint.

A centrifugal juicer spins quickly via the power provided by its motor and is faster to use and easier to clean. Some people worry that it may heat the juice a little bit and diminish the content level of raw enzymes. In my experience with the centrifugal juice of the juice still comes out cool so I would like to think that we are retaining the majority of the enzymes we need.

A press juicer is something where you manually press the juice out of vegetables and fruits. It's a completely heat free process and so it may retain raw enzymes better, although I don't think it makes a huge difference. Press juicers are more challenging to clean and they take a lot longer to use.

So, if you're looking for a practical answer you might choose a centrifugal juicer. Make sure you look at how many of the pieces are able to be placed in the dishwasher if that is something that may be more compelling to you. Look at ease of cleaning. And choose a juicer with multiple speeds. Here's my opinion on why: if you have a high and a low speed available in your juicer it's easier for you to juice greens and herbs.

Your high-speed switch on your centrifugal juicer will be great for things like carrots, beets, large fruits, celery, cucumbers. Anything big. When you deal with leafy greens like spinach or kale or herbs you'd like to include you need to be able to use a low speed. You also need to fill the reservoir where the produce is placed before you start the juicer. Otherwise, the greens will just fly around and not be juiced because a centrifugal juicer spins very fast. That's the centrifugal part! And because little spinach leaves or pieces of kale or mint are very light they will fly around in a circle and not get pressed into the juicing mechanism. So you need to fill the reservoir with greens and use the piece where you press the produce down into the juicing mechanism to hold the leaves in place before you start the juicer on low. You can check out my Instagram and YouTube channel, both under my name, Amy Leigh Mercree, for more in depth how-to videos on how this works. And if you post videos yourself juicing please hashtag them so I can share them! Use the hashtag #chakrasandcrystalscookbook.

"I heart juicing." Amy Leigh Mercree #chakrasandcrystals cookbook #veganjuicing

Smoothies Are Spectacular

Smoothies are a burst of nutrients as well! Some of these provide you with all the vitamins and minerals and enzymes that we talked about in our juicing chapter plus all of the added fiber from the produce. They are as easier to digest as a juice but fiber is also a critical aspect of our digestion. It keeps things moving and flowing and it also provides us with crucial prebiotics, which are the food for the probiotics or healthy intestinal bacteria and flora that we have naturally.

To make your smoothies you can use any blender you like and you can also use your blender or food processor to make the sorbets discussed in our cookbook. I love to make a smoothie for breakfast and it's unbelievably delicious and nutritious. I almost think of it like dessert for breakfast!

To up the nutritional value of the smoothies in this book you can always add your favorite vegan protein powder. You can even add that to your sorbets! That might take delicious fresh sorbet and make it an appropriate dinner some nights. Because it will be full of protein and vitamins and minerals.

Chakra Affirmations While You Cook

You will notice each recipe starts off with a wonderful affirmation for that chakra. Make sure you say it aloud as you create the food you will be eating or the drink you will be drinking to empower that chakra. You can continue to use our affirmation throughout the day to really enhance the energy of the chakra upon which you're focusing.

"*Conscious eating
is the new
master cleanse.*"
Amy Leigh Mercree
#chakrasandcrystals
cookbook

ROOT CHAKRA RECIPES

rooted

grounded

secure

strong

.

Root Chakra Rooted Beet Juice

"I am stable, secure, and grounded. I am deeply connected to the abundant earth below me."

Serves: 2

Ingredients:
4 beets (skin on, scrubbed)
Beet greens (from the four beets used)
1/2 inch piece of ginger
1 lime
2 cucumbers
1 handful of cherries (pits removed)

Juice the above ingredients for a root chakra empowering blast of nutrients!

Root Chakra Cherry Rose Smoothie

"I am rooted in the Earth. My feet feel enlivened and secure on the ground below me."

Serves: 2

Ingredients:
1 small bag of frozen cherries, pits removed
4 cups of almond milk
Dash of stevia or 1 tablespoon of honey
1/4 cup of goji berries
1 tiny sprinkle of cayenne pepper (optional)
2 organic red rose petals

Blend the cherries, almond milk, and sweetener of your choice in a blender until smooth. Garnish with goji berries, one rose petal each, and the cayenne pepper on top.

Root Chakra Pomegranate Grape Ruby Jewels Salad

"My root chakra is nourished and strong. It is a shining ruby jewel at my base."

Serves: 2

Ingredients:
1/2 cup red grapes, cut in half
1/4 cup pomegranate seeds
1 cup peeled and cubed beets
1 cup peeled and cubed turnips
6 tablespoons of olive oil
1/3 cup sprouted adzuki beans
1/4 cup chopped fresh thyme
1 cup arugula
4 cups of assorted chopped greens or lettuce
Thinly sliced pieces of 1 parsnip
1/4 cup of chopped walnuts
Juice of 4 limes
1 teaspoon ginger juice
Sea salt to taste
Organic bee balm flower petals

Get ready for a flavor flash in your mouth with this sweet, tangy, and savory salad.!
Sauté the beets and turnips in 2 tablespoons of olive oil until cooked though with edges lightly browned.
Mix 4 tablespoons of olive oil, the lime juice, the ginger juice, the fresh thyme, and sea salt and set aside to dress the salad.
Toss all of the ingredients (except the flower petals) including the cooked beets, turnips, and the dressing. Sprinkle the bee balm petals on top and enjoy!

Elderflower Astragalus
Smoky Quartz Crystal Infusion

"I am present in the moment. My attention is here."

Serves: 2

Ingredients:
1 teaspoon dried astragalus
1 teaspoon dried elderflower herb
Drizzle of honey
8 ounces of hot water
Smoky quartz piece(s)

Put the astragalus and elderflower in a ceramic mug and pour the hot water over it and cover for 10 minutes. Place the smoky quartz pieces up against the edge of the mug to let the energy of the minerals steep with the herbs.
Strain out the astragalus and elderflower. Add a drizzle of honey.
Hold the smoky quartz as you sip the herbal infusion and repeat the affirmation above.

"Connection to the earth is the root of all abundance."
Amy Leigh Mercree
#chakrasandcrystals
cookbook

SACRAL CHAKRA RECIPES

creative

sensual

fluid

pleasure

Sacral Chakra Peachy Pleasure Juice

"Creativity flows through my body like an endless river of light."

Serves: 2

Ingredients:
2 peaches (halved with pits removed)
2 nectarines (halved with pits removed)
6 strawberries
4 carrots
1 apple

Juice the above ingredients for a sacral chakra enlivening blast of nutrients!

Sacral Chakra Sweet Life Sorbet

"I embrace the sweetness of life with my whole body."

Serves: 2

Ingredients:
3 cups of frozen mango
1 cup frozen strawberries
2 figs
Drizzle of maple syrup
1/4-1/3 cup of apple juice
Pinch of organic calendula petals

Put the figs in the blender and whirl to pulverize. Next add the mango and strawberries and a little bit of apple juice. Run blender briefly. Turn off blender and once it stops use a spoon and bring the bottom fruit to the top. Replace cover and blend again. Repeat until mostly smooth adding a little juice as needed. You want to keep the mixture as thick as possible. Once it is blended transfer into cups and drizzle with syrup and sprinkle with calendula petals.

Sacral Chakra Orange Squash Salad

"My sacral chakra is full of light and joy."

Serves: 2

Ingredients:
1 tablespoon of roasted and salted pumpkin seeds
1 tablespoon of roasted and salted cashew halves
1 cup peeled and cubed butternut squash
1 cup peeled and cubed acorn squash
1 chopped persimmon
1/4 cup squash blossoms
1/2 cup of orange juice
1 large bunch of basil
4 cups of mixed greens
2 tablespoons olive oil
Pinch of sea salt

Sauté the butternut squash, acorn squash in 2 tablespoons of olive oil until cooked though with edges lightly browned. Add the squash blossom flowers at the end to lightly steam. Remove from heat and sprinkle with sea salt. Put the orange juice and basil in the food processor and blend until smooth.
Toss all of the ingredients together (except the orange basil dressing) including the cooked squashes. Then drizzle with the dressing and serve.

Calendula Maca Carnelian Crystal Infusion

"My healthy sensuality is nourishing and enhancing."

Serves: 2
Ingredients:

1 teaspoon dried calendula
1 teaspoon maca powder
Drizzle of maple syrup
8 ounces of hot water
Carnelian and/or orange calcite piece(s)

Put the calendula and maca in a ceramic mug and pour the hot water over it and cover for 10 minutes. Place the mineral pieces up against the edge of the mug to let the energy of the minerals steep with the herbs.
Strain out the calendula. Add a drizzle of syrup.
Hold the stones as you sip the herbal infusion and repeat the affirmation above.

"The ocean of creativity within you can be an endless source of pleasure."
Amy Leigh Mercree
#chakrasandcrystals
cookbook

SOLAR PLEXUS RECIPES

confident

successful

powerful

independent

Solar Plexus Chakra
Independence Incarnate Juice

"I am confident, powerful, and successful."

Serves: 2

Ingredients:
1/2 of a lemon
10 stalks of fennel
1 peeled pineapple

Juice the above ingredients for a solar plexus chakra blast of powerful nutrients!

Solar Plexus Chakra Banana Confidence Smoothie

"My body is radiant and filled with power."

Serves: 2

Ingredients:
3 cups of frozen banana
2 cups of rice milk
Drizzle of honey
1 starfruit
1 tablespoon of melissa flowers

Combine the bananas, rice milk, and starfruit in a blender until smooth. Serve and garnish with a drizzle of honey and the melissa flowers on top.

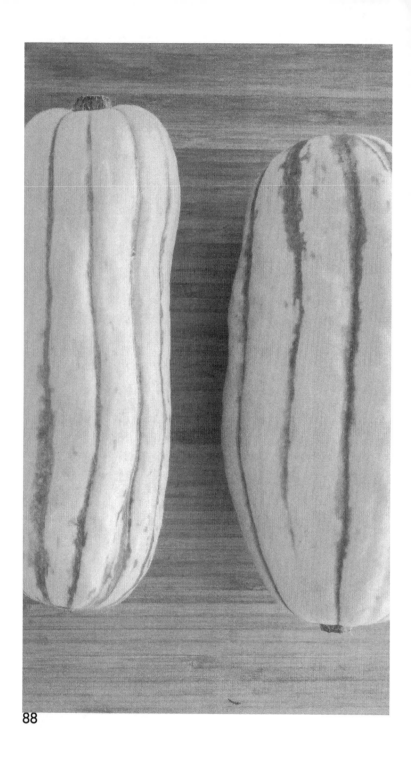

Solar Plexus Chakra Chickpea Fennel Salad

"My solar plexus chakra is bright and clear."

Serves: 2

Ingredients:
1 tablespoon of canned chickpeas
2 stalks of fennel, sliced thin
1 cup sliced delicata squash
1/2 cup chopped artichoke hearts
1 fresh corn on the cob
1/4 cup dill flower blossoms
1/4 cup of lemon juice
1 small, chopped bunch of dill
4 cups of mixed greens
7 tablespoons olive oil
Sea salt to taste
1 teaspoon ground turmeric

Prepare a cookie sheet with 3 tablespoons of olive oil and preheat to 350 degrees.
Cut the delicata squash in half and deseed. Then slice thin. Place in single layer on cookie sheet.
Vertically slice the corn off of the corncob and place it on the cookie sheet in a single layer.
Place the chickpeas in a single layer on the cookie sheet.
Sprinkle everything on the cookie sheet with ground turmeric and sea salt. Bake for 30 minutes at 350 degrees.
Put the orange juice and basil in the food processor and blend until smooth.
Toss all of the cooked and raw ingredients together and enjoy!

Marshmallow Citrine Crystal Infusion

"My divine will is aligned with the highest good."

Serves: 2

Ingredients:
1 teaspoon dried marshmallow leaf
Drizzle of honey
8 ounces of hot water
Citrine and/or amber piece(s)

Put the marshmallow leaf in a ceramic mug and pour the hot water over it and cover for 10 minutes. Place the citrine and amber pieces up against the edge of the mug to let the energy of the minerals steep with the herbs. Strain out the marshmallow leaf. Add a drizzle of honey. Hold the stones as you sip the herbal infusion and repeat the affirmation above.

"Be confident in your dreams. Your happiness & fulfillment are worth the effort."
Amy Leigh Mercree
#chakrasandcrystals
cookbook

HEART CHAKRA RECIPES

loving

compassion

romantic

caring

Heart Chakra Mint Green Juice

"Compassion flows through my body like an endless river of love."

Serves: 2

Ingredients:
1 bunch of spinach
1/2 bunch of mint
1/2 bunch of parsley
4 stalks of celery
1 bunch of bok choi
1 pear
1/2 bunch of chard
1 zucchini

Juice the above ingredients for a heart chakra love blast!

Heart Chakra Loving Compassion Sorbet

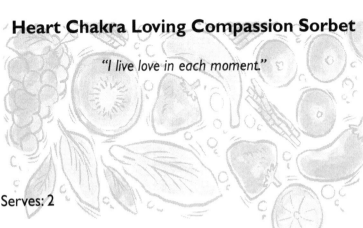

"I live love in each moment."

Serves: 2

Ingredients:
5 cups of frozen green grapes
1/4-1/3 cup of cold steeped green tea
1/4 cup of fresh mint leaves

Add the green grapes, mint and a little bit of green tea to the blender. Run blender briefly. Turn off blender and once it stops use a spoon and bring the bottom fruit to the top. Replace cover and blend again. Repeat until mostly smooth adding a little tea as needed for desired consistency. You want to keep the mixture as thick as possible. Once it is blended transfer into cups and garnish with mint leaves.

Heart Chakra Gorgeous Green Salad

"My heart chakra is full of love and caring."

Serves: 2

Ingredients:
1 tablespoon of chopped fresh chives
1 tablespoon of chopped fresh scallions
1 chopped broccoli head
1/4 cup mung bean sprouts
1/4 cup of lime juice
1 small bunch of chopped kale
4 cups of spinach
1/2 cup of thawed and dried frozen peas
1/2 cup chopped celery
1/2 cup arugula
2 tablespoons olive oil
Pinch of sea salt to taste

Toss all of the ingredients together and serve.

Emerald Heart Crystal Infusion

"My heart is open and full of love."

Serves: 2
Ingredients:

1 green tea bag
1 jasmine tea bag
8 ounces of hot water
Rose quartz, malachite, jade, and/or adventurine piece(s)

Put the tea bags in a ceramic mug and pour the hot water over it and cover for 10 minutes. Place the mineral pieces up against the edge of the mug to let the energy of the minerals steep with the herbs.
Serve.
Hold the stones as you sip the herbal infusion and repeat the affirmation above.

"Truly open your heart to love & set sail on an endless shimmering sea of happiness."
Amy Leigh Mercree
#chakrasandcrystals
cookbook

THROAT CHAKRA RECIPES

well-spoken

communicative

expressive

respected

Throat Chakra Watermelon Expression Juice

"When I speak, the world listens."

Serves: 2

Ingredients:
4 cups of watermelon, rind removed
1 cup of boysenberries
1 cucumber
1 bunch fresh mint

Juice the above ingredients for a throat chakra opening treat. Serve and garnish with fresh mint.

Sublime Communication Sorbet

"I easily express myself and feel aligned with those around me."

Serves: 2

Ingredients:
4 cups frozen blueberry
1/2 cup red currant
2/3 cup brewed herbal tea of your choice (try naturally decaffeainated tea substitue rooibos or naturally sweet licorice root!)
1/2 teaspoon of finely chopped dried or fresh lemongrass

Put the blueberries and currants and a little bit of tea in the blender and run it briefly. Turn off blender and once it stops use a spoon and bring the bottom fruit to the top. Replace cover and blend again. Repeat until mostly smooth adding a little juice as needed. You want to keep the mixture as thick as possible. Once it is blended transfer into cups and sprinkle with lemongrass.

Throat Chakra Blueberry Salad

"My throat chakra is full of power and ease."

Serves: 2

Ingredients:
1 tablespoon of slivered almonds
1 tablespoon of roasted and salted sunflower seeds
1 cup cubed blue potatoes
1 cup blueberries
1/4 cup squash blossoms
1 large bunch of basil
4 cups of mixed greens
6 tablespoons olive oil
Pinches of sea salt to taste
1 shallot, peeled and chopped finely
1/3 cup red currants
2 tablespoons of lime juice

Sauté the blue potatoes and shallots in 2 tablespoons of
olive oil until cooked though with edges lightly browned.
Sprinkle with sea salt.
Put the red currants, the rest of the olive oil, the lime juice
and half of the basil in the food processor and blend until
smooth.
Toss all of the ingredients together (except the red currant
basil dressing) including the cooked potatoes. Then drizzle
with the dressing and serve.

Licorice Lemongrass Lapis Lazuli
Crystal Infusion

"My healthy communication is effortless and enhancing. I listen to others and truly hear them."

Serves: 2
Ingredients:
1 teaspoon dried licorice root or a licorice tea bag
1 teaspoon fresh lemongrass, sliced thin
8 ounces of hot water
Lapis lazuli, blue lace agate, larimar and/or angelite piece(s)

Put the licorice and lemongrass in a ceramic mug and pour the hot water over it and cover for 10 minutes. Place the mineral pieces up against the edge of the mug to let the energy of the minerals steep with the herbs.
Strain out the loose herbs.
Hold the stones as you sip the herbal infusion and repeat the affirmation above.

"Express yourself & be empowered. You're a unique treasure & your ideas matter."
Amy Leigh Mercree
#chakrasandcrystals
cookbook

BROW CHAKRA RECIPES

intuitive

clear-seeing

awakened

psychic

Brow Chakra Psychic Currant Juice

"My intuition guides me to my highest good."

Serves: 2

Ingredients:
4 cups of blackberries
1 cup of black currant
2 cucumbers
1 bunch fresh mint

Juice the above ingredients for a brow chakra opening treat. Serve and garnish with fresh mint.

Blackberry Intuition Smoothie

"I sense the world around me and am in tune with my intuition."

Serves: 2

Ingredients:
4 cups frozen blackberries
4 cups almond milk
1/2 cup of finely chopped dark chocolate

Put the blackberries and almond milk in the blender and blend thoroughly. Once it is blended transfer into cups and stir in the chocolate.

Brow Chakra Blackberry Salad

"My brow chakra is clear seeing and well protected."

Serves: 2

Ingredients:
1 tablespoon of chopped walnuts
1 tablespoon of pine nuts
1 cup blackberries
1/4 cup hyssop petals
1 large bunch of mint
4 cups of mixed greens
6 tablespoons olive oil
Pinches of sea salt to taste
2 tablespoons of grape juice
2 tablespoons of wine (optional)

Whisk the olive oil, the grape juice, sea salt, and wine for the dressing.
Toss all of the ingredients together and serve.

Gingko Labradorite Crystal Infusion

"My intuition is easy and enhancing. I see clearly and I feel psychically safe."

Serves: 2

Ingredients:
1 gingko tea bag
8 ounces of hot water
Labradorite, violet fluorite, sugalite piece(s)

Put the ginko in a ceramic mug and pour the hot water over it and cover for 10 minutes. Place the mineral pieces up against the edge of the mug to let the energy of the minerals steep with the herbs.

Hold the stones as you sip the herbal infusion and repeat the affirmation above.

"Use your intuition and see the truth in all situations."
Amy Leigh Mercree
#chakrasandcrystals
cookbook

CROWN CHAKRA RECIPES

guided

connected

spiritual

angelic

Crown Chakra Dandy Detox Juice

"My spirit and body are infused with radiant light."

Serves: 2

Ingredients:
4 cups of dandelion greens
2 plums
4 cucumbers

Juice the above ingredients for a detoxifying crown chakra treat.

Lavender Plum Smoothie

"My crown chakra is alive with joy and divine guidance."

Serves: 2

Ingredients:
4 cups frozen plums (cut plums in half and remove pit, then freeze)
4 cups almond milk
1/2 teaspoon of finely chopped dried lavender

Put the plums and almond milk in the blender and blend thoroughly. Once it is blended transfer into cups and sprinkle with lavender.

Crown Chakra Asian Violet Salad

"My crown chakra is empowered and well protected."

Serves: 2

Ingredients:

1 cup of sliced daikon radish

2 cups of sprouts of your choice

1 cup dandelion greens (chopped)

1 large cucumber (chopped or sliced)

6 cups of spinach greens

6 tablespoons sesame oil

Pinch of sea salt to taste

3 tablespoons of lime juice

1 tablespoon ginger juice

20 violet flowers with stems still attached, untreated with chemicals

1 1/2 cups water

1 cup granulated sugar

1/4 tsp almond extract or 1 Tsp rosewater (optional)

Fine sugar (to sprinkle)

Wash the violets gently. Use a spray bottle and very lightly mist the violets in a colander. Leave the stems on the violets. Let them dry for a few minutes.

Place the granulated sugar, water and almond extract or rosewater in a pan and heat until the sugar is completely dissolved, stirring frequently.

Gently dip each flower in the sugar water using small tongs or tweezers. Place on wax paper. Sprinkle liberally with the fine sugar. Next cut the stems off and let the violets dry in a cool place with low humidity.

Whisk together the sesame oil, the lime and ginger juices, and sea salt for the dressing.

Toss all of the ingredients, except the candied violets, together. Place in serving bowls and then sprinkle liberally with the violets and enjoy.

Lavender Amethyst Crystal Infusion

"My spiritual connection is strong and clear. I am my higher self and I am lovingly guided by angels and archangels."

Serves: 2

Ingredients:
1 teaspoon dried lavender
8 ounces of hot water
A pinch of dried, powderderd stevia
Amethyst, clear quartz, howlite piece(s)

Put the lavender in a ceramic mug and pour the hot water over it and cover for 10 minutes.
Place the mineral pieces up against the edge of the mug to let the energy of the minerals steep with the herbs.
Strain out the lavender and add the stevia.
Hold the stones as you sip the herbal infusion and repeat the affirmation above.

"You are guided by an endless array of benevolent, nonphysical helpers. Just say yes to them."
Amy Leigh Mercree
#chakrasandcrystals
cookbook

NOT THE END -
BUT A BEGINNING

I am so honored that you have taken this journey with me! I hope that you have made so much delicious food and drink that you feel empowered and enhanced. I hope that your chakras are glowing and spinning like the beautiful wheels of light they are. And I hope that your entire light body is flowing like the series of beautiful rivers of lights that I know it is. I wish you a life of peace, joy, and endless luminous love.

This book is a new beginning. It opens the door for you to choose a life where conscious eating nourishes you and enhances everything you encounter. Your body will thank you. And your spirit will soar. Remember, cooking is an adventure! Embrace the color, texture, and vitality food can bring you!

To download your FREE Chakra Toolkit and power up all of your chakras right now go to www.amyleighmercree.com/chakratoolkit - password CHAKRAS

BIBLIOGRAPHY

"Agastache hybirda 'Astello Indigo.'" Seedaholic.com. Accessed August 3, 2016. http://www.seedaholic.com/agastache-hybrida-astello-indigo-2872.html

"Bougainvillea Essence." The Healing Garden. Accessed August 3, 2016. http://the-healing-garden.me.uk/2015/08/bougainvillea-essence/

Deane, Green. "Edible Flowers: Part Eight." Eat the Weeds. Accessed August 3, 2016.
http://www.eattheweeds.com/edible-flowers-part-eight/

"Health Benefits of Lemon Verbena." Organic Facts. Accessed August 3, 2016.
https://www.organicfacts.net/health-benefits/herbs-and-spices/lemon-verbena.html

Jackson, Deb and Karen Bergeron. "Bee Balm, Wild Bergamot, Herb Uses and Medicinal Properties." Alternative Nature Online Herbal. Accessed August 3, 2016. https://altnature.com/gallery/beebalm.htm

Ji, Sayer. "Black Seed: The Remedy for Everything But Death." GreenMed Info. Last modified January 3, 2013. http://www.greenmedinfo.com/blog/black-seed-remedy-everything-death

"Lemon Balm/Melissa." Herbwisdom. Accessed August 3, 2016.
http://www.herbwisdom.com/herb-lemon-balm.html

Stradley, Linda. "Edible Flowers Chart." What's Cooking America. Accessed August 3, 2016. http://whatscookingamerica.net/EdibleFlowers/EdibleFlowersMain.htm

"Soul Food: Dandelion for the Root Chakra." That Good Ish. Last modified December 26, 2014. https://thatgoodish.wordpress.com/2014/12/26/dandelion-root-for-the-root-chakra/

The Crystal Healing Shop. "How to Use Crystals." Accessed July 21, 2016. http://crystalhealingshop.com/how-to-use-crystals/

Dean, Benjamin. "How do Healing Crystals Work? Healing with gemstones, how it works." Emily Gems. Accessed July 20, 2016. http://crystal-cure.com/article-how-healing-crystals-work.html

Energy Muse. "How to Make Your Own Crystal Grid." Last modified March 29, 2016. http://www.energymuse.com/blog/crystal-grids/

Energy Muse. "Learn the Meanings of Healing Gemstones." Accessed July 21, 2016. https://www.energymuse.com/about-gemstones

The Ancient Sage. "Herbs and Crystals for the Chakras." Accessed July 24, 2016. http://www.theancientsage.com/herbs-and-crystals-for-the-chakras/

Baldwin, Sarah. "5 Herbs to Heal the Sacral Chakra." Spirits Voice, LLC. Accessed July 25, 2016. http://spiritsvoice.com/5-herbs-to-heal-the-sacral-chakra/

Harton, Robyn A. "A to Z Crystal Meanings." Crystals and Jewelry.com. Accessed July 25, 2016. http://meanings.crystalsandjewelry.com/a-to-z-list-of-crystal-meanings/

in5d: Esoteric Metaphysical Spiritual Database. "7 Herbs for 7 Chakras." Last modified January 12, 2015. http://in5d.com/7-herbs-for-7-chakras

Medicine Hunter. "About Adaptogens." Last modified 2012. http://www.medicinehunter.com/adaptogens

Scialla, Janelle. "Chakra Crystal Chart." Crystal Healing. Last modified June, 2008. http://www.crystal-healing.org.uk/crystal-healing/chakras-and-colour-therapy/chakra-crystal-chart

Virtue, Doreen and Robert Reeves, N.D. "20 Spiritual Herbs for Activating Higher Consciousness, Awakening Intuition, and Deep Healing." Conscious Lifestyle Magazine. Accessed July 25, 2016. http://www.consciouslifestylemag.com/spiritual-herbs-plants-healing/

Eostre Organics. "Organic Food: Sustainable and Healthy Food Production." Accessed October 6, 2016. http://www.eostreorganics.co.uk/

PubMed.gov. "Pesticides and Cancer." https://www.ncbi.nlm.nih.gov/pubmed/9498903

RECOMMENDED READING

A Little Bit of Chakras by Chad and Amy Leigh Mercree

A Little Bit of Buddha by Chad Mercree

Joyful Living: 101 Ways to Transform Your Spirit and Revitalize Your Life by Amy Leigh Mercree

Adventures for Your Soul by Shannon Kaiser

The Soul Searcher's Handbook by Emma Mildon

The Spiritual Girl's Guide to Dating by Amy Leigh Mercree

Find Your Happy by Shannon Kaiser

Sacred Success by Barbara Stanny

The Way of the Psychic Heart by Chad Mercree

Love is in the Earth by Melody

Move Your Stuff Change Your Life by Karen Rauch Carter

Angel Tech by Antero Alli

The Untethered Soul by Michael Singer

The Compassion Revolution: Thirty Days of Living from the Heart by Amy Leigh Mercree

A Little Bit of Meditation by Amy Leigh Mercree

Amy Leigh Mercree's motto is "Live joy. Be kind. Love unconditionally." She counsels women and men in the underrated art of self-love to create happier lives. Amy is a bestselling author, media personality, and medical intuitive. Mercree speaks internationally focusing on kindness, joy, and wellness.

Mercree is the bestselling author of "The Spiritual Girl's Guide to Dating: Your Enlightened Path to Love, Sex, and Soul Mates," "A Little Bit of Chakras: An Introduction to Energy Healing," "Joyful Living: 101 Ways to Transform Your Spirit and Revitalize Your Life," "The Chakras and Crystals Cookbook: Juices, Sorbets, Smoothies, Salads, and Crystal Infusions to Empower Your Energy Centers," and "The Compassion Revolution: 30 Days of Living from the Heart."

Mercree has been featured in Glamour Magazine, The Huffington Post, Aspire Magazine, Your Tango, Spirituality & Health Magazine, LA Yoga Magazine, AOL Latina, Soul and Spirit Magazine, Women's Health and Inc. Magazine.

Check out AmyLeighMercree.com for articles, picture quotes and quizzes. Mercree is fast becoming one of the most quoted women on the web. See what all the buzz is about @AmyLeighMercree on Twitter, Snapchat and Instagram.

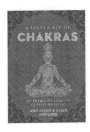  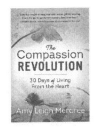

Stay tuned for "The Spiritual Girl's Guide to Dating Expanded Anniversary Edition" and "A Little Bit of Meditation" in 2017!

Reshape your inner world
through 21 days of
free chakra balancing

https://amyleighmercree.leadpages.co/
dailychakrabalancing/

http://amy-leigh-mercrees-products.myshopify.com/

ROCK YOUR CHAKRAS
A Transformational Online Course to Empower Your Energy Centers
with
Amy Leigh Mercree

AmyLeighMercree.com/rockyourchakras

The Rock Your Chakras 7 Day Course will help you to...

Get your love life working well through clearing blocks in your Sacral and Heart Chakras

Energize your body for optimum health through balancing your chakras

Attract abundance into your life through being an open energy channel

Awaken your creativity and connect you with experiences that bring you joy

Ignite your passion for life, and for love

Attract the right kind of people into your life who will make life even more enjoyable for you

MEET YOUR GUIDES
1-2-1 Skype Session with Amy Leigh Mercree

Ever wondered where your gut feelings come from? Or that little voice in your head that knows what is about to happen? Learn who your life guides are and hear their guidance. Ask them questions and open your intuitive senses in this fun and enlightening session.

MEDICAL INTUITIVE SESSION
1-2-1 Skype Session with Amy Leigh Mercree

Amy has been a practicing Medical Intuitive for over 15 years. As a medical intuitive she uses extra-sensory skills to intuit the cause of bodily dis-ease. Dis-ease can be actual disease but also smaller harder to diagnose ailments, and notably, the precursors of disease before they became known. Medical Intuitive work is great for prevention and tuning up of your health and for new ways to clear health issues.

Amy looks at the energy of your body like a grid and identifies 'hot spots', blockages, densities, and issues ready to be integrated. The emotional, mental and ancestral origins of these issues are often discovered and Amy's wide array of original Medical Intuitive Protocols reprogram your body for optimum health.

Many more types of sessions available at:

http://amyleighmercree.com/work-with-amy/

145

LET'S GET SOCIAL

Let's meet up online

I love to connect with new friends.

follow me on
goodreads

@amyleighmercree